GIVE *ideals* THIS CHRISTMAS . . . Let *ideals* express your heartfelt wishes at every season of the year!

Every issue of **Ideals** is bursting with a celebration of life's special times: Christmas, Thanksgiving, Easter, Mother's Day, Country and Friendship. Give a gift subscription to **Ideals** this Christmas and you will bring joy to the lives of special people six times a year! Each issue offers page after page of magnificent photographs, exquisite drawings and paintings, delightful stories and poetry. Each is a "keeper" that invites the reader back, again and again, to look, read and ponder. There's nothing quite as special as a gift of **Ideals**!

WE'LL SEND A GIFT ANNOUNCEMENT WITH THE FIRST ISSUE!

SAVE 44%
off the bookstore price!
To order, mail card below or call toll-free
1-800-558-4343

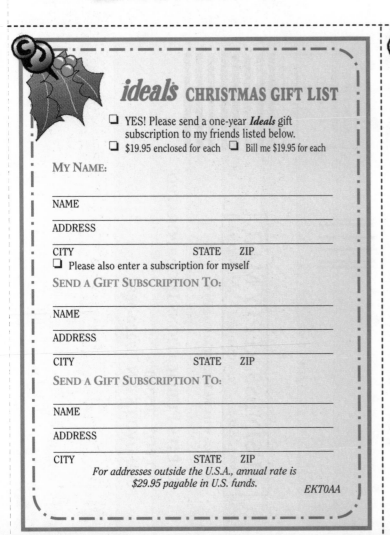

ideals CHRISTMAS GIFT LIST

❑ YES! Please send a one-year *Ideals* gift subscription to my friends listed below.
❑ $19.95 enclosed for each   ❑ Bill me $19.95 for each

MY NAME:

NAME

ADDRESS

CITY   STATE   ZIP
❑ Please also enter a subscription for myself

SEND A GIFT SUBSCRIPTION TO:

NAME

ADDRESS

CITY   STATE   ZIP

SEND A GIFT SUBSCRIPTION TO:

NAME

ADDRESS

CITY   STATE   ZIP
For addresses outside the U.S.A., annual rate is $29.95 payable in U.S. funds.
EKT0AA

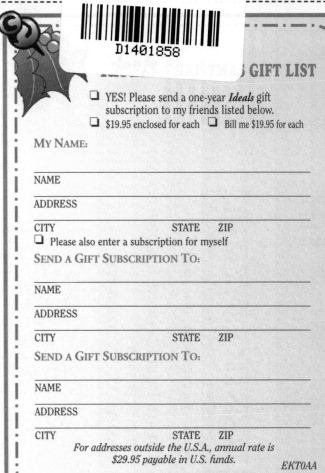

ideals CHRISTMAS GIFT LIST

❑ YES! Please send a one-year *Ideals* gift subscription to my friends listed below.
❑ $19.95 enclosed for each   ❑ Bill me $19.95 for each

MY NAME:

NAME

ADDRESS

CITY   STATE   ZIP
❑ Please also enter a subscription for myself

SEND A GIFT SUBSCRIPTION TO:

NAME

ADDRESS

CITY   STATE   ZIP

SEND A GIFT SUBSCRIPTION TO:

NAME

ADDRESS

CITY   STATE   ZIP
For addresses outside the U.S.A., annual rate is $29.95 payable in U.S. funds.
EKT0AA

Do your Christmas shopping today and SAVE 44%

off the regular bookstore price of *Ideals* when you give a one-year subscription!

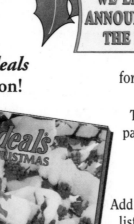

Everyone knows at least two or three people who would love a gift subscription to *Ideals*! It's a very special Christmas gift that keeps on reminding a close friend or relative of your thoughtfulness all through the year. And, when you order now, you enjoy a generous savings off the regular bookstore price—and do your Christmas shopping right away!

WE'LL SEND A GIFT ANNOUNCEMENT WITH THE FIRST ISSUE!

ONLY $19⁹⁵

for each one-year gift subscription of six issues— a savings of $15.75 off the bookstore price.

To order today, use one or both of the postage-paid reply cards (see reverse side) or call toll-free

1-800-558-4343

Add more gifts, if you wish, by enclosing a separate list with the additional names and addresses and mailing in an envelope to:

Ideals Publications, Inc.
P.O. Box 305300, Nashville, TN 37230

SEND NO MONEY NOW—WE'LL BILL YOU LATER!

Orders received after December 1 will start with the Easter issue.

ideals®

THANKSGIVING

More Than 50 Years of Celebrating Life's Most Treasured Moments

Vol. 57, No. 5

Joy is the grace we say to God.
—*Jean Ingelow*

IDEALS—Vol. 57, No. 5 September MM IDEALS (ISSN 0019-137X)
is published six times a year: January, March, May, July, September, and November by
IDEALS PUBLICATIONS, a division of Guideposts,
535 Metroplex Drive, Suite 250, Nashville, TN 37211.
Periodical postage paid at Nashville, Tennessee, and additional mailing offices.
Copyright © MM by IDEALS PUBLICATIONS, a division of Guideposts.
POSTMASTER: Send address changes to Ideals, PO Box 305300,
Nashville, TN 37230. All rights reserved.

Title IDEALS registered U.S. Patent Office.
SINGLE ISSUE—U.S. $5.95 USD; Higher in Canada
ONE-YEAR SUBSCRIPTION—U.S. $19.95 USD; Canada $36.00 CDN (incl. GST and shipping); Foreign $29.95 USD
TWO-YEAR SUBSCRIPTION—U.S. $35.95 USD; Canada $66.50 CDN (incl. GST and shipping); Foreign $55.95 USD

Subscribers may call customer service at 1-800-558-4343 to make address changes.
Unsolicited manuscripts will not be returned without a self-addressed, stamped envelope.

ISBN 0-8249-1163-6   GST 893989236

Visit *Ideals*'s website at www.idealspublications.com

Cover Photo
BOUNTIFUL HARVEST
Jane Wooster Scott, artist
Image from Superstock

Inside Front Cover
GATHERING LEAVES
William Trost Richards, artist
Image from Christie's Images

Inside Back Cover
THAT'S ME PUMPKIN
John George Brown, artist
Image from Christie's Images

Autumn Days
Will Carleton

Yellow, mellow, ripened days,
Sheltered in a golden coating;
O'er the dreamy, listless haze,
White and dainty cloudlets floating;
Winking at the blushing trees
And the somber, furrowed fallow;
Smiling at the airy ease
Of the southward-flying swallow.
Sweet and smiling are thy ways,
Beauteous, golden autumn days!

Quiet Day
May Smith White

This is the quiet day I long have sought,
When burnished leaves hang mutely
on each tree.
Here is true beauty, still untouched, unsought—
These scenes will live throughout eternity.
The autumn wind grows silent with her song,
Like birds that cease their calls at end of day;
And one forgets that time was ever long
As yearning minds follow the last sunray.

True glory comes to every waiting heart;
As when the busy earth is brought to rest,
The fading rose adds to this timeless art
And waits the artist's brush to here attest.
Each autumn sings with joy still unsurpassed,
The present one more glorious than the last.

Both mums and goldfish bring out the rich hues of autumn in this Greenville, Indiana, garden. Photo by Daniel Dempster.

Autumn's Beauty

May Smith White

I cannot let these autumn days slip by
Without recalling one who loved them so,
The one who always watched October sky
Bend down to meet the evening's western glow.
This time renews the past, and I recall
Again this one who always went to see
The first ripe acorns in the early fall,
The browning leaves that drifted from each tree.

Now autumns come, it seems, more frequently,
And each one leaves a trace upon my mind
To stir again a dream now dimmed to me,
A pattern, lost, which I shall never find.
But, like this one who loved the quiet days,
I too must know the good of autumn ways.

Autumn Festival

Ethelyn M. Kincher

These friendly hills are now attired
To dance to tunes by winds inspired;
Each golden tree will swing and sway
With oakbrush dressed another way.
Confetti leaves will fill the air;
Ripe apples will be royal fare;
The harvest moon will shed its light,
So dancing can go on all night.

But when the festival is through,
The friendly hills find rest is due.
And so in ermine robes they keep
A rendezvous with healing sleep.

Right: In rural Missouri, the bounty of harvesttime is on display for photographer Gay Bumgarner.
Overleaf: South Falls plunges into the Silver Creek Canyon below in Oregon's Silver Falls State Park. Photo by Terry Donnelly.

October

Gladys Taber

The wild geese went over early one morning this week. Why this is so moving, I do not know. All of us feel it; in the village store someone says, "I heard the geese go over," and there is a moment of silence. We seldom make much of the swallows or other migratory birds when they leave, although we are very likely to note the redwings when they come back in March. But the geese—ah, that is to feel a quickening of the heart.

High and lovely, they wedge through the sky, their faint cries drifting down to earth, and for a brief time we seem to fly too. How do they chart their course? How many miles do they travel? How many of them fail to make it? How do they know when they've reached their destination? And how high do they fly? Perhaps higher than other birds.

Days grow shorter now, the nights chillier. Crisp mornings call for buttermilk pancakes and maple syrup, with country sausage on the side; at supper the popovers are almost too hot to hold. The trees kindle with color, a few at a time: small flashes of scarlet appear in the swamp, and the sugar maples begin to glow as the great wave of autumn glory slowly rises to full tide. Leaves start to fall; I pick one up. It is cool to the touch; a hint of pink lies under the gold. As it dries, the serrated edges curl inward and the leaf turns to tawny brown. I think, I am holding autumn in my hand.

As the trees give up their summer finery, the world around me comes into view once more. I can see the postman stopping at the mailboxes along the road, the lights at suppertime glowing in

Artist Winifred Marie Louise Austin captures a familiar yet favorite autumn sight in BRENT GEESE IN FLIGHT. *Image from Christie's Images.*

kitchen windows. It is pleasant to have my horizon widened again! I always *know* Willie and Wilma are just around the bend on Jeremy Swamp Road, but it's nice to *see* neighbors' rooftops and chimneys and windows.

Where only a month ago the valley was clothed in emerald, it is now clad in mustard gold, peppery red, and nutmeg brown. The cockers jump and roll in heaps of leaves and then dash into the house, where they shed autumn drifts of color on the rug and hearth. When Teddy flings himself into a carefully raked pile of leaves, he vanishes up to his eyebrows. It takes him no more time at all to demolish one hour's work!

Roadside stands splash more color along the roads now, and I wish I could paint them. Great smoky blue Hubbard squash, dark green acorn squash, bright-orange pumpkins, strings of Chinese lanterns, baskets of rosy apples and bouquets of bit-tersweet, and sometimes Indian corn and gourds—all make a carnival of autumn and testify to nature's endless bounty. Jugs of freshly pressed cider stand in the cool shade, as well as jars of clover honey. Sometimes there are new-laid eggs for sale, or homemade jellies, lucent in the sun, or rich preserves and jars of crisp pickles, and sometimes loaves of fresh homemade bread and pans of crusty rolls. It is fun to stop to visit with the men who keep the stands and talk crops and gardens. And when you arrive home, the back seat is full of special things you just couldn't resist buying. . . .

I reflect that nothing really ends, but grows into something new. The harvest is in and the leaves will all be down soon, but they enrich the ground, and new leaves will put forth tender green in spring, in the endless cycle of nature. Today is a part of time, a unit, but it evolved from yesterday and flows into tomorrow like a tide.

Readers' Reflections

Hickory Treasures

Zann Vickers Easterwood
Martin, Tennessee

The golden treasury of autumn
Found in October days,
The richness of the harvest's
Warming sunshine rays.
A yellow butterball moon
Dresses the black velvet sky;
Winds hold a kiss of frost
As ducks and geese begin to fly.
Soon there will be bonfires,
Their orange blaze to warm beside.
The scampering storing squirrels—
The hickory tree is a treasure box inside.
And all the world prepares
To snuggle under toasty covers.
The wonderful days of harvest—
Such a delight for October lovers.

Whenever October Comes Over the Hill

Nora M. Bozeman
Nixa, Missouri

Whenever October comes over the hill
She spills her red and gold at will.
She covers summer's flowery days
With copper-colored leaf displays.

She autumn-dresses every tree
In cloaks of crimson artistry.
She skips among the trees and then
Spreads golden sunshine on the glen.

October's days are bittersweet,
Too soon they leave on padded feet.
So, my cup of red and gold I'll fill
Whenever October comes over the hill.

Waltz

Evelyn Heinz
McHenry, Illinois

Rust, orange, and burgundy—
Colored leaves of
Autumn danced away

When the cold
Northwest wind
Waltzed in today.

A yellow-leaved maple
Slipped out of
Her autumn dress.

Being hugged and
Twirled by
Winter's caress.

God's Golden Treasures
Linda C. Grazulis
Pittsburgh, Pennsylvania

Autumn once again is blazing
With its colors bright and bold,
Such a time of joy and laughter,
Treasures of purest gold.

Fields are abundant with the harvest
Of pumpkins orange and round;
Cobs of corn have fallen
Upon the leafy ground.

The harvest moon is beaming
As owls gather near the barn;
Pheasants and turkeys strut their stuff,
Displaying all their charms.

A dreamy breeze of autumn
Blows gently on the face
While the leaves of oaks and maples
Tiptoe about the land with grace.

Sassafras and sumac
Are a few treasures from autumn's chest;
But, oh, the crimson of the oak tree
Reveals autumn at its best!

Only God could've created
Such a rainbow-colored sight,
From goldenrod to ginkgo's fan
And geese which now take flight!

Falling Leaves
Evelyn Steen Taylor
Monroe, Louisiana

The falling leaves tell me
That autumn is near;
The wind sounds its music
That bids me to hear.

Briskly it blows
As the leaves twirl and fly,
Guiding their descent
As they spin their goodbye.

With splendor they lived;
The sun made them thrive.
Rain brought a freshness,
Keeping them alive.

Now the season dictates,
The time soon will come
To rest upon the earth;
The winter is upon.

We feel not a sadness;
Their beauty we behold.
As they turn loose the branches,
The sky turns to gold.

Editor's Note: Readers are invited to submit unpublished, original poetry for possible publication in future issues of Ideals. Please send typed copies only; manuscripts will not be returned. Writers receive $10 for each published submission. Send material to Readers' Reflections, Ideals Publications, 535 Metroplex Drive, Suite 250, Nashville, Tennessee 37211.

Eternal Gardener

Eunice M. Vigil

September has greeted October,
And summer rubs elbows with fall.
The hummingbird darts in the garden,
Reluctant to part with it all.

My work in the soil is near over,
The pruning and mulching soon through.
And tucked in with each little pansy
Is a bit of eternity too.

I'll do what I must for the roses
And tidy the lichen wall
That cradles the violet and primrose
And tenderly yield them to fall.

When God planned His beautiful Eden
And walked His great garden alone,
There was surely a fair weeping willow
Near a wall made of lichen stone.

I care not for mansions nor riches,
Nor places where jewels abound.
Dear Lord, in the vastness of heaven,
Just save me one small plot of ground.

*Hydrangea blooms reveal subtle autumn color
in this photo by Steve Terrill.*

> The mellow
> autumn came,
> and with
> it came
> the promised
> party to
> enjoy its
> sweets.
>
> —George Gordon,
> Lord Byron

Gathering Pawpaws

May Allread Baker

We hunted pawpaws in the quiet wood
One early, mild autumnal afternoon
And found a loveliness surpassing June
In purple beech and russet oak. We stood
Upon a slope where pines grew tall and old
And mosses flourished in their solemn shade
While in their lofty tops the breezes played,
And sunshine trickled down in drops of gold.

Then presently we wandered through the vale
Where sumac flung its scarlet banners out
And found at last the half-forgotten trail
And saw the pawpaws growing all about.

The luscious fruit was yellow, flecked with mauve;
We filled our basket in the leafy grove.

In Autumn, Fruits

Anya P. Sala

We do not seek to gather fruits in spring
Before the petals drop from fertile blooms
And fruits have formed where now those petals cling—
(A season intervenes ere fruiting comes).
Nor do we doubt there will be fruits in time
When first we see the branches stark and bare.
Our faith presumes that when the interim
Of growing ceases, fruit shall be hanging there.
Believing this, we rush our nascent dreams
To premature completion and we rail
Against a fate which shrivels half-formed schemes—
If seasons will not rush, can man prevail?
Spring is the season planned for dreams and growing;
In autumn, fruits of harvesting—and knowing.

Pawpaws and crimson leaves dot the ground in Missouri. Photo by Gay Bumgarner.

From My Garden Journal

Deana Deck

CONCORD GRAPES

As a child, I spent many summer weeks and holidays visiting my grandparents in a little country town named El Reno, Oklahoma. They lived in a 1930s house located on an unpaved street at the very edge of town. The house and its surrounding yard contained everything a child might enjoy: a wrap-around porch with a swing, huge oak trees to climb, a frog pond, and an old tractor on which to sit. I marveled at all of these, but my favorite attraction was a trellis laden with Concord grapevines that was located behind the house and right next to the frog pond. The trellis, too low to sit under to enjoy shade, was just the right height from which to pluck grapes, even if you were only seven years old and barely four feet tall.

My brother and I, along with our cousins, always spent two weeks with Grandma and Granddad in the early summer and several days at Thanksgiving. During our summer visit, the unripe grapes were small and green, too sour to eat, but perfect for plucking and lobbing at frogs in the pond. It was part of our morning routine to pick a handful of grapes and take turns climbing onto the old tractor seat, where we were magically trans-

formed into Air Corps bombardiers with Frog City in our sights. The frogs didn't eat the grapes, nor did they seem to mind being used as targets. They just hopped out of the way.

Every once in a while, just out of curiosity, one of us would eat a grape. We had been warned that green grapes would make us sick; but of course we didn't believe it until the stomach cramps started. After that, we were content just to chew on them for a while to extract their sour flavor and then spit them out. Even when green, the inside lining of a Concord grape skin gives a hint of what's to come when they turn purple and succulent.

One year, my family made an unusual late-summer trip to El Reno. It was the first time I had been there when the grapes were ripe, and I savored the plump Concord grapes warm off the vine. As their skin slipped off and left a mound of sweet fruit in my mouth, their taste rivaled the purest grape juice I could imagine. All of those years of tasting only green grapes seemed to heighten my appreciation for the ripe Concords' flavor.

Once the Concord grapes reached this perfect state of flavor, my grandmother would begin making her famous grape jelly. Grandma had spent many an autumn day in her hot kitchen mastering the jelly-making process. At Thanksgiving dinner, she usually offered us the first taste of her efforts, served on homemade biscuits. She generously shared her jelly throughout the holidays but always saved enough for peanut butter sandwiches and morning toast during our summer visits.

Memories of those sweet Concord grapes and Grandma's delicious jelly have stayed with me through the years. When I moved into my own house fifteen years ago, I planted several two-year-

CONCORD GRAPES

old Concord grapevines my first week there. I bought several gardening books to learn how to prune and cultivate them. The books instructed me that grapes only form on one-year-old wood, so older canes need to be removed and the current season's wood shortened so that only a few buds remain. This process allows for a healthy harvest of plump grapes the following season, rather than a huge harvest of puny grapes that season.

To protect the young Concord vines, I spread weed barriers under them to keep wild strawberries, chickweed, and other intruders from sucking nutrients away from their roots. I mulched them with pine bark to maintain well-balanced soil; and throughout the spring, I fed them nourishing meals of compost and manure washed down with plenty of water. During dry periods, I laid a soaker hose at their base so the soil could stay moist but not wet. When the vines grew longer, I built a small trellis, much like the one on my grandparents' property, that provided support and allowed critical air circulation.

In their third spring, the vines rewarded my hard work with blossoms—tiny blossoms of delicate pink touched with green. Little bunches of green balls began to appear, which occasionally I'd chew; the memories of those long-ago Oklahoma summers flooded back. Slowly, the green balls transformed in size and color until they looked like grapes. In preparation for my harvest, I started reading cookbooks and studying how to make grape jelly and grape juice; I was ambitious and highly optimistic.

One day I looked at the vines and knew that the harvest was near. Each bunch had several grapes that were turning a deep purple. The next day, I eagerly returned to see their progress but found there were no more purple grapes left—lots of green but no purple. This continued for days

I savored the plump Concord grapes warm off the vine. Their taste rivaled the purest grape juice I could imagine.

until I discovered the birds, mostly bluejays, were plucking off the ripest grapes. To deter my feathered friends, I bought a package of bird netting. I climbed a ladder and carefully spread the netting around the vines, fastening it at the bottom so no bird would find a way in.

Finally, after having nurtured and protected my vines for so long, I was rewarded with several pounds of ripe grapes. Harvesting them was difficult because the tendrils, by which grapevines hold on to the trellis, were now entangled in the bird netting. I had to cut away pieces of the net to reach the grapes, but in light of my juicy harvest, I did not mind the additional labor.

I ate handfuls of grapes and put the rest into a kettle to begin the jelly-making process. I cooked and stirred, and cooked and stirred some more, ever anticipating the jewel-filled jars that would soon line my pantry shelves. But I soon realized just how much my harvest of grapes had been reduced by bluejays and boiling. After two summers, countless hours of cultivation, a couple of hours of netting and un-netting, and several more hours of cooking and stirring, I finally had my prize: three measly jars of grape jelly.

I had planned to give my jars of Concord grape jelly away as Christmas gifts; but after all my hard work, I decided to keep the three jars and enjoy them myself. I felt I had earned the pleasure, and I knew no one would appreciate each bite as much as I. The experience filled me with renewed respect for my grandmother, stirring and stirring in her unair-conditioned kitchen so that her grandchildren could add sweet Concord grape jelly to the long list of things for which we were thankful.

Deana Deck tends to her flowers, plants, and vegetables at her home in Nashville, Tennessee, where her popular garden column is a regular feature in The Tennessean.

TORCHES
Berniece Ayers Hall

Thank You, God, for autumn trees
On dark hills that burn
Like bold torches. Oh, from these
There is much to learn.
When October winds have swept
Down with chilling blast,
Wise and patient trees have kept,
Treasuring till last,
Then to lavish gold and red
Like a living flame.
Thus with beauty earth is fed
As the hills proclaim
Praises 'neath a cheerless sky.
So in autumn, Lord, would I.

THE POPLARS' FLAME
Joy Belle Burgess

Now is the bright and shining hour
When gleaming tapers light the lane,
When the yellow leaves of poplars
Fill the sky with quivering flames.
For the trees are tall and dazzling,
Fully garmented in light,
And the morning sun ascending
Is more beautiful and bright.

The country lane is gilded
By their lovely glow on high
As they lift their boughs of splendor
And their statures touch the sky.
Now fanned by gentle breezes,
Their flames leap high and bright;
And the autumn lane is mellowed
By their glowing, tender light.

A golden poplar tree stands before a hillside of fall foliage.
Photo by William Johnson/Johnson's Photography.

Boy Making a Jack-o'-Lantern

Grace V. Watkins

One eye's a trifle oversize?
The nose is tipped a bit?
The teeth look miscellaneous
As though they don't quite fit?
Don't tell your son his sculpturing
Would rate a feeble C
Or pry the knife away from him
And wield it skillfully;
But give him an affectionate smile,
Approve his budding art
That there may be success upon
His face and in his heart.

First Pumpkin

Dan A. Hoover

Down in Grandpa's patch of pumpkins,
Warm skies over all,
Frosty Halloween has painted
Red-gold leaves of fall.
Grandson picked the largest pumpkin,
Ridged and orange-red;
Made his grandpa puff to lift it
To the wagon bed.
Grandpa cut his teeth, some missing,
Two triangular eyes;
Grandson bounced around with pleasure,
Laughed with pleased surprise.
Candle placed within the center,
Glowing warm and bright.
Grandpa knew he'd always smile
Remembering that night.

A grandfather offers a carving lesson to two eager youngsters in Jack-o'-Lantern *by artist Abbot Fuller Graves (1859–1936). Image from Christie's Images.*

Look for Things

Edna Jaques

Look for things to be thankful for:
A dear old face at an open door,
The table set for the family meal,
A husband's love that is true as steel.

A cushioned chair that you fixed yourself,
Your favorite books on a nearby shelf,
A green-hued twilight that sort of glows,
The clean, fresh smell of a brier rose.

An old windjammer that you recall
Beating its way through an April squall,
Its old sides crusted with salty spray,
Limping in at the close of day.

The lovely odor of lemon peel;
A humble man with a flaming zeal
For a worthy cause that he thinks is right;
The feeling of warmth on a winter night.

Look for things to be thankful for:
A braided rug on your bedroom floor,
A dormer window with curtains drawn,
A bluebird singing across the lawn.

So much to be thankful for these days,
So much to enjoy and love and praise.

Guests for Thanksgiving dinner are greeted by a festive front entry at this home in Ohio. Photo by Jessie Walker.

TRANSITION

Steven-Adele Morley

One by
One by
Twos and
Threes
The petals
Fall from
Off the trees.
Crimson, yellow,
Orange, maize,
Red and bright
Before my gaze.
Transfixed I stand
More hypnotized
Than if I stared
Into the eyes
Of some great master.
Here today the softened
Breeze
That paints the garnet
In the leaves;
But gone tomorrow will they be,
Leaving but the barren tree.

THE CITY OF FALLING LEAVES

Amy Lowell

Leaves fall,
    Brown leaves,
Yellow leaves streaked with brown.
They fall,
    Flutter,
    Fall again,
    The brown leaves
And the streaked yellow leaves
    Loosen on their branches
    And drift slowly downward.
    One,
    One, two, three,
    One, two, five.
All Venice is a falling of autumn leaves,
Brown, and yellow streaked with brown.

LEFT: Two young boys gather pumpkins, apples, and memories. Photo by Barbara Peacock/FPG International.
BORDER: Leaves from a Chinese Dove tree cover the ground in Seattle, Washington. Photo by Terry Donnelly.

Devotions FROM THE Heart

Pamela Kennedy

It is of the Lord's mercies that we are not consumed, because his compassions fail not. They are new every morning: great is thy faithfulness. Lamentations 3:22–23

GREAT IS THY FAITHFULNESS

I needed an idea. It was early morning and I was starting my daily walk, so I quickly whispered a prayer for God to give me an inspiration to use as a Thanksgiving meditation for the women's group at church. The air was filled with the scent of tropical flowers. Birds called to one another in the branches of the mango trees, and a gentle breeze rustled the palms. Our home rests on a volcanic hillside on the eastern side of Oahu, Hawaii, a place rich in natural beauty. As I strode energetically down the sidewalk, I felt the wind change and become stronger. By the time I reached the bottom of the hill, turned, and began the mile-long walk back up, I could see the dark clouds, driven by the trade winds rolling over the mountaintop. Soon misty veils of rain advanced toward me, and within minutes I was being drenched in a tropical shower. As I trudged, soaked and dripping, back up the hill, I was a sorry sight: hair plastered to my face, shirt flapping like a wet sail, shoes squishing with each step. By the time I reached the hilltop, I was chilled despite the exertion.

The rain slackened, and I turned for a moment to glance back down into the valley. It was at that moment God answered the rushed prayer I had whispered as I left home. Stretched across the valley, framed by an expanse of sapphire sea and emerald hillside, was a brilliant rainbow. Suddenly, the words of a favorite hymn filled my mind:

Summer and winter, and springtime and harvest,
Sun, moon, and stars in their courses above,
Join with all nature in manifold witness,

> *Dear Father, I give thanks to You now and always for Your faithfulness. Because of it, I can face each day knowing all will be well. Amen.*

To thy great faithfulness, mercy, and love.
Great is Thy faithfulness! Great is Thy faithfulness!
Morning by morning new mercies I see.
—Thomas O. Chisholm, 1923

The words reminded me to give thanks for God's faithfulness that renews and redeems life in constant cycles. Rainstorms are followed by rainbows; night is followed by day; winter is followed by spring; and inevitably, after sorrow, joy returns. I thought of the times when I had felt trapped in darkness, fearful that nothing would change. But one day, I realized that the light had indeed returned—God is ever faithful. This was the message I could share at Thanksgiving!

With a new spring in my step, I made the last turn in the road and headed for home. As I approached my house, my neighbor came out to the mailbox; she was dressed for work, stylish in a tailored skirt and blouse. She stopped short and let out a deep laugh as she saw me slogging along, a trail of damp footprints testimony to my encounter with what we islanders call a "*mauka* shower."

"Looks like you picked the wrong morning to go for a walk!" she called in a good-natured tone.

"Oh, no," I answered, stopping to wring some of the water from my hair. "It was the most perfect morning for a walk you could ever imagine."

A rainbow forms in the crashing waves at Oregon's Shore Acres State Park. Photo by Dennis Frates/Oregon Scenics.

Autumn

Amy Carmichael

Great giver of my lovely green in spring,
A dancing, singing green upon my tree,
My green has passed; I have no song to sing,
What will my autumn be?

Must it be, though alive, as all but dead,
A heavy-footed and a silent thing?
Effectless, sapless, tedious, limited,
A withered vanishing?

Thus I; but He to me: Have I not shown
In autumn woodland and on mountain fell,
The splendor of My purpose for Mine own?
Fear not, for all is well.

And thou shalt see, My child, what I will do,
For as thy lingering autumn days unfold,
The lovely, singing green of hitherto
Will come to thee in gold.

*The sun glistens through the golden branches of a sugar maple
in Brown County, Wisconsin. Photo by Darryl R. Beers.*

THANKSGIVING

Isla Paschal Richardson

We thank God for so many things today.
Though some may call them little things, yet we
Have learned we cannot measure blessings nor
The stars just by the viewpoint that our eyes see.

For friendly neighbors, for a gleaming hearth,
For strength to serve the ones we love each day,
For laughter and contented comradeship,
Our gratitude for these is poor repay.

For eyes that see His hand where beauty is,
For faith that holds fast to man's brotherhood,
For hope and courage, and through tears and smiles,
Abiding confidence that God is good.

Now looking back on joys and blessings past
(Though some perhaps may never come again!),
I am so thankful that when they were mine
My heart was deeply grateful for them then.

Gratitude is the fairest blossom
which springs from the soul;
and the heart of man knoweth
none more fragrant.
—Hosea Ballou

The fruits of a farmer's labor create a colorful mosaic in
this photo by John Michael/International Stock.

THROUGH MY WINDOW

Pamela Kennedy

Art by Eve DeGrie

EMPTY POCKETS

I teach high school girls. Each semester I get a new batch, but they are remarkably alike. Oh, they look different from one another, and they come in a variety of sizes and shapes, but they almost all share a common accessory—a pocketful of complaints. "My brother never has to do anything." "I have to do everything." "My parents won't trust me." "My nose is too big." "My hair is too thin." "I'm ugly." "I'm stupid." "I'm a mess!" It's a litany familiar to many who know teenagers, but I suspect there are lots of adults with pockets full of complaints as well. "My family doesn't appreciate me." "My kids never listen to me." "My house is

too small." "My hips are too wide." "I'm exhausted." "I'm bored." "I'm a wreck!"

The first day of each semester I tell a story I heard long ago. It's a parable that bears repeating, especially at this time of year.

A single mother and her daughter lived in an apartment outside a small town. Each morning, as the mother headed for work at a local diner, she picked up a little tablet, and throughout the day she jotted notes on slips of paper. As she walked home each night, she leafed through the tablet, tore out the sheets, and placed each in either the right or left pocket of her coat. After dinner, the daughter watched as her mother emptied her pockets and silently read the scribbling on the papers. The mother's shoulders inevitably slumped and her lips settled into a grim line; it seemed to the daughter that the light went out of her mother's eyes as she read the mysterious notes. Life in the lonely apartment was quiet and joyless.

One evening while the two were eating supper, the girl asked her mother about the notes. "Does someone give you the notes that make you so unhappy, Mother?" she inquired.

"Oh, no," replied the older woman, "I write them to myself. Each day I take this small tablet to work. All day long I jot down notes about what I see and hear and what people say to me. On the way home I tear off the sheets of paper and place the good things in my right coat pocket and the bad things in my left pocket. Then, at the end of the day, I review all my notes and recall the kind of day I had."

The daughter was puzzled. If what her mother said was true, why was she always so sad at the end of each day? Surely some good things happened to her mother. The girl decided to investigate, and the next night, as soon as her mother began to prepare supper, the daughter went to the closet. She pulled out her mother's coat and plunged her hand into the left pocket. Sure enough, there were half a dozen small sheets of paper. She quickly read through them: cheap tipper, bus was late, boss chewed me out, cook mixed up orders, customer swore at me, burned hand on coffee pot, tore dress. Replacing the notes, the girl then reached into the other pocket, but it was empty. She felt around more carefully, and her fingers touched the ragged edges of fabric. The seam at the bottom of the pocket was completely torn away. Thoughtfully, the daughter withdrew her hand and returned the coat to its hanger.

After the meal was finished, the mother completed her evening ritual of reviewing her day and went to bed. The daughter, however, took out her small sewing basket and retrieved her mother's coat from the closet. She carefully sewed together the bottom edges of the right-hand pocket. When she was finished, she tested it with her hand to ensure that the stitches were strong. Then she took

her scissors and just as carefully snipped the bottom seam from the left coat pocket. Smiling, she replaced the coat in the closet and went to bed.

The next night, as the mother reviewed her notes, a smile played across her lips. Her shoulders straightened, and the furrows on her tired brow smoothed. "Let me tell you about the funny thing that happened today," she said as her daughter cleared the supper dishes. Soon the two of them were giggling over the antics of an eccentric customer.

Later that night, as the daughter knelt beside her bed to pray, she whispered softly, "Thank You, God, for empty pockets."

When I finish telling the story, I explain to my students that they will be writing in journals at the beginning of each class day and that they will be required to write down two things for which they are grateful at the end of each day's entry. At first this little exercise is difficult for some, but within a week or so it is interesting to observe how they begin to notice the simple joys in their lives. A good breakfast, a smile from a friend, a teacher who allowed an extra day to finish a report, a dad who brought ice cream home for dessert—all become remembered blessings. By the end of the semester, each student has been introduced to the habit of gratitude.

I don't think teenagers are the only ones who need to hear this story of the empty pockets. So many of us let the good things, the small blessings of each day, pass by unremembered as we store up and rehash every hurt, slight, and grudge. What better time than now to rip the seams from pockets of sorrow and release the things that weigh down our hearts? Let us resolve instead to ponder the blessings of life, the common joys of nature, and the rich abundance of friends and family. This Thanksgiving may our pockets overflow with gratitude.

Pamela Kennedy is a freelance writer of short stories, articles, essays, and children's books. Wife of a retired naval officer and mother of three children, she has made her home on both U.S. coasts and currently resides in Honolulu, Hawaii.

Renovated Church

Amelia Evans Mix

The dome is white, preserved since days of old,
The work of our forefathers' loyal hands.
Old walls are white, the molding band of gold.
Soft carpeting is tufted violet strands.
Three chandeliers lend brilliance from their height.
Large stained-glass windows, holding every hue,
Reflect the sun with restful controlled light
On faces in each soft, gold-cushioned pew.
The grand old organ peals out; renovated,
It's gained more volume and a better tone.
The choir, in purple robes, rejuvenated,
Sings out. The minister stands there alone;
With God, he hopes the light of each soul gleams
Like sunshine through stained glass, fulfilling dreams.

A Church Spire

Enid Martell Olson

Something there is about a lofty spire
That shakes the very heart of me;
I know not why.

For I have seen it rise against the morning sky,
Startling against the splendor of the rose-dipped clouds;
And I have felt the hope of newborn day.

And I have seen it point into a slate-gray dawn,
Sturdy against the scudding of the blue-winged clouds;
I felt its strength despite the shifting winds.

I saw the steeple soar into a cloudless noon,
Silver against the glory of the burning blue;
I felt the freedom of a boundless space.

I saw its lifted cross above the prairie's rim,
A silhouette against the golden western sky;
I knew the promise of the setting sun.

And when I saw the draperies of the northern lights
Touching the spire with a sweeping, silken hem,
I felt the awesome majesty of heaven.

But deep within me I will not forget
(No matter where I am in years to come)
A pine tree and the steeple of a church
Framed in a stained-glass window looking east.

Perhaps God placed them there
That every day and hour
I might remember
He was near.

A church in Cornwall Bridge, Connecticut, raises its spire to the morning sky. Photo by Chuck Schmeiser/Unicorn Stock Photos.

Let Us with a Gladsome Mind

John Milton

Let us with a gladsome mind
Praise the Lord, for He is kind;
For His mercies aye endure,
Ever faithful, ever sure.

He, with all commanding might,
Filled the new-made world with light;
For His mercies aye endure,
Ever faithful, ever sure.

He the golden-tressed sun
Caused all day his course to run;
For His mercies aye endure,
Ever faithful, ever sure.

The hornéd moon to shine by night,
'Mid her spangled sisters bright;
For His mercies aye endure,
Ever faithful, ever sure.

All things living He doth feed;
His full hand supplies their need;
For His mercies aye endure,
Ever faithful, ever sure.

Let us with a gladsome mind
Praise the Lord, for He is kind;
For His mercies aye endure,
Ever faithful, ever sure.

Above: A doe pauses on the edge of the forest in this photo by Scott Barrow/International Stock.
Right: A footbridge arches across the Roaring River in Linn County, Oregon. Photo by Steve Terrill.

A SLICE OF LIFE

Edgar A. Guest

GRACE

Dear Lord, for food and drink and peace
And all that makes our day so fair,
And for the evening's sweet release
From duty and its round of care
Once more we turn to Thee above,
Acknowledging Thy boundless love.

Dear Lord, in every blossoming tree,
In every bloom our garden knows,
Thy marvelous handiwork we see,
Thy love we find in every rose.
Lord, may the service which is ours
Reflect Thy glory as the flowers.

Be with us through this night, we pray,
And make our little circle strong;
May none among us go astray.
Help us to choose the right from wrong.
Within these walls, however tried,
May love and friendliness abide.

Edgar A. Guest began his illustrious career in 1895 at the age of fourteen when his work first appeared in the Detroit Free Press. His column was syndicated in more than three hundred newspapers, and he became known as "The Poet of the People."

PAT THOMPSON

Thanksgiving

Bertha A. Kleinman

The brown leaves fall, and under all
The tiny seeds are living,
But cannot speak; how much they seek
To join in our Thanksgiving.

They love Thee, Lord, but have no word
To tell how they adore Thee.
And unto me the task shall be
To sing my song before Thee.

The lilies grow and this I know,
Their beauty is Thanksgiving.
Their hearts of gold in praise unfold
To tell the joy of living.

They love Thee, Lord, but have no word
To tell how they adore Thee.
And unto me the task shall be
To sing my song before Thee.

*The colors of autumn are captured in a
bouquet in this photo by Nancy Matthews.*

Thanksgiving Inventory

Sudie Stuart Hager

I thank Thee, Lord, for beauties such as these
Out of the dying year's abundant yield:
The first long strands on weeping-willow trees,
The rich brown furrows of a new-plowed field.

Sunset clouds like chariots of fire,
A mountain lake of deep, mysterious blue,
Exultant music of a linnet choir,
The scent of roses, cool and fresh with dew.

Frost-turned maples in a hilltop row,
Bins of corn and dancing bonfire lights,
Arms of cedars sagging under snow,
Drifts of wind-blown stars on clear, cold nights.

I thank Thee, Lord, for beauties given me;
I pray I gave some lovely thing to Thee.

The Pilgrim

John Bunyan

Who would true valor see,
Let him come hither!
One here will constant be,
Come wind, come weather;
There's no discouragement
Shall make him once relent
His firm-avowed intent
To be a Pilgrim.

Whoso beset him round
With dismal stories,
Do but themselves confound;
His strength the more is.
No lion can him fright;
He'll with a giant fight;
But he will have a right
To be a Pilgrim.

Nor enemy, nor friend
Can daunt his spirit;
He knows he at the end
Shall life inherit:
Then, fancies, fly away;
He'll not fear what men say;
He'll labor, night and day,
To be a Pilgrim.

An image from a nostalgic greeting card celebrates Thanksgiving. Image from Sol Novinsky/Superstock.

OUR HERITAGE

A MODELL OF CHRISTIAN CHARITY

John Winthrop, 1630

Thus stands the cause betweene God and us, we are entered into Covenant with him for this worke, wee have taken out a Commission. . . . the Lord will be our God and delight to dwell among us, as his owne people and will commaund a blessing upon us in all our wayes, soe that wee shall see much more of his wisdome power goodnes and truthe then formerly wee have beene acquainted with, wee shall finde that the God of Israell is among us, when tenn of us shall be able to resist a thousand of our enemies, when hee shall make us a prayse and glory, that men shall say of succeeding plantacions: the lord make it like that of New England: for wee must Consider that wee shall be as a Citty upon a Hill, the eies of all people are uppon us; soe that if wee shall deale falsely with our god in this worke wee have undertaken and soe cause him to withdrawe his present help from us, wee shall be made a story and a by-word through the world, wee shall open the mouthes of enemies to speake evill of the wayes of god and all professours for God's sake; wee shall shame the faces of many of god's worthy servants, and cause theire prayers to be turned into Cursses upon us till wee be consumed out of the good land whether wee are goeing: . . . wee are Commaunded this day to love the Lord our God, and to love one another to walke in his wayes and to keepe his Commaundements and his Ordinance, and his lawes, and the Articles of our Covenant with him that wee may live and be multiplyed, and that the Lord our God may blesse us in the land whether wee goe to possesse it: . . . Therefore lett us choose life, that wee, and our Seede, may live; by obeyeing his voyce, and cleaveing to him, for hee is our life, and our prosperity.

ABOUT THE TEXT

"A Modell of Christian Charity" was written by John Winthrop in 1630 while he and other Puritans sailed from Southampton, England, to Massachusetts. Winthrop, who was elected governor of the Massachusetts Bay Colony prior to the voyage, preached this text in the form of a sermon shortly before the Puritans' arrival in America. In this excerpt, Winthrop admonishes the Puritans to maintain a covenant with God and their fellow man and to recognize that they are a "City upon a Hill," with the eyes of the world upon them. Winthrop's commitment to providing spiritual leadership for the Puritans as they began life in the New World helped to establish faith as a guiding principle of our country.

The Pilgrims and Native Americans share food and fellowship in THE FIRST THANKSGIVING 1621 *by artist Jean Leon Gerome Ferris (1863–1930). Image from Superstock.*

The Plymouth Apple Declined

H. F. Gould

Visiting at the house of a friend in Boston, I was shown an apple which he told me had been sent to him from Plymouth, and was the fruit of a tree that was planted by Peregrine White, the first child born of Pilgrim parents in New England. I praised the apple for its beauty and the venerable associations connected with it. He wished me to keep it; but, as he had no other of the tree, I declined the gift.

I wanted the apple, when offered to me
    By its generous owner, but thought it not right
To take it, because it had grown on a tree,
    That sprang from a seed sown by Peregrine White.
And he, who thus proffered it, had none beside it;
While diffidence checked the words, "Let us divide it."
Now Peregrine White was the first child, you know,
    Who drew his first breath in New England—the child
Whose parents were making to bud and to blow,
    With its earliest blossoms, America's wild:
But he with the fruit never questioned me whether
We might partake of the apple together.
Though a fabled divinity once had let fall
An apple of gold, where his favorites thronged,
Inscribed, "Of the fair, to the fairest of all!"
    It was not to me this whole apple belonged:

My friend was no god—and then I, but a woman;
I thought that to halve it were just about human.
The whole I declined; still I did not deny
    A wish that, unuttered, was strong in my heart;
And from it entire, while averting my eye,
    I own I was secretly coveting part;
And had he divided the offering presented,
Preserving one half, I had come off contented.
Had Solomon been there to put in a word,
    His wisdom had brought the debate to an end,
Deciding at once, by the edge of his sword,
    This contest of kindness between friend and friend.
Yet he with the apple was quite too short-sighted
To see how I might in a half have delighted.
I hope that next autumn he'll go where it grew,
    And, if not forbidden the fruit, that he'll reach
And pluck a fair apple, then cut it in two
    And tell me at once that a half is for each.
Of friendship's best gift how the worth may be lightened
By having it whole, when, if shared, how 'twere heightened!

In Apple Harvest *by artist Levi Wells Prentice (1851–1935), a bushel basket offers plenty of ripe apples to share. Image by Christie's Images.*

Nancy Skarmeas

JAMES FENIMORE COOPER

James Fenimore Cooper, America's first successful novelist, wrote prolifically for more than thirty years of his life; although, family tradition has it that Cooper began writing on a whim. He was fond of reading aloud to his wife and children in the evenings, and after reading a passage from a new and unimpressive English novel, he is said to have exclaimed, "I could write you a better book myself!" Cooper's daughter later recalled that her mother laughed incredulously at her husband's boast, reminding him that he was known as an unenthusiastic letter writer. But Cooper was true to his word and immediately set about writing a novel, *Precaution*, which was published in 1820. *Precaution* was a dismal failure, the worst possible imitation of the

least popular English fiction of the day. Cooper, however, was inspired rather than discouraged by his failure; he refused to give up his writing experiment so easily. In fact, he would never give it up at all. For the remaining three decades of his life, James Fenimore Cooper was to be a writer by trade.

James Fenimore Cooper was born in 1789 in Burlington, New Jersey, but his childhood was spent in upstate New York, near Lake Otsego. Cooper's father was a wealthy local judge, and the family lived a comfortable life; nonetheless, they lived on what was then the frontier, and the sights and sounds and characters of frontier life provided Cooper with his earliest memories and rich experiences which would later provide the backdrop for the stories and novels of his adult years.

Cooper traveled a diverse road before beginning his career as a writer. After attending an Albany boarding school, he matriculated at Yale; but he was expelled for his involvement in a prank. He then turned toward the sea; he first tried to get work on a ship and then signed on with the United States Navy. In the navy, Cooper twice sailed to England; he later served in Lake Ontario and New York City before resigning his commission in 1811 to marry Susan Augusta De Lancey.

Troubles plagued the Coopers for several years. After the death of Cooper's father, there ensued a lengthy and bitter battle over the estate. Cooper became, due to the subsequent death of his older brother, responsible for more people and more debt than his income could manage. It was at this point of financial uncertainty that Cooper took up his writing experiment.

In planning his second novel, Cooper heeded the advice of his wife and closest friends, the same advice that has been given to writers throughout history.

Write what you know, they told him. As logical as this directive may seem, it was a radical idea in 1820s-America. Critics and writers alike were in agreement that American audiences had no interest in reading the work of one of their own countrymen, especially not if that countryman intended to write about American life and characters. Few truly American novels had yet been written, and none had met with any great financial success. British themes and British style were considered the standard against which all writers of fiction were measured.

Cooper had experimented with British themes and style, yet he had failed. An amateur writer with little to lose, he decided to break with convention on his second book. He based his plot on a story told to him by former Continental Congressman John Jay. Cooper called his novel *The Spy*, and in it he fleshed out Jay's story with legend, lore, and history gleaned from conversations with his upstate New York neighbors, many of whom had fought in and witnessed the Revolutionary War. The results were phenomenal. *The Spy* was the most popular American novel yet written, one that went on to unheard of second and third printings. Cooper had fulfilled the promise to his wife; he had written a "better book" and in so doing had broken ground on a new genre of American fiction.

Cooper went on to become America's most beloved novelist. Knowing a good thing when he came upon it, he continued to explore distinctly American themes. He wrote about the lasting legacy of the Revolutionary War. He wrote of the difficulty of dealing with the Native Americans. He wrote about American characters and American history, about woodsmen, sailors, and pioneers. In his five-volume series known as the *Leatherstocking Tales*, which includes *The Last of the Mohicans*, Cooper wrote about life on the edge of the frontier. In other novels he wrote about American adventurers at sea. Whenever he put pen to paper, Cooper heeded the advice that had launched his career; he made his native country his subject.

As Cooper neared the end of his life, his literary star dimmed as the sky filled with other, brighter lights. In the decades after Cooper's greatest success

as a writer, Nathaniel Hawthorne, Herman Melville, and Mark Twain all laid claim to the American novel, each with more lasting critical success than Cooper. In light of this new American fiction, critics began to see Cooper's novels as simplistic and overly didactic. Mark Twain even chronicled Cooper's missteps as a novelist in a humorous essay entitled "Fenimore Cooper's Literary Offenses." But as much as Twain laughs at Cooper, the detail of his essay also proves that he read Cooper and read him carefully. Whether or not Twain wanted to admit it, Cooper's work influenced and helped shape his own.

James Fenimore Cooper died in 1851. To this day, his books continue to be read and taught and studied, and his characters and scenes of pioneer America still have a hold on the national imagination. Natty Bumppo, the protagonist of the *Leatherstocking* novels, has been called by at least one scholar "one of the greatest characters in fiction"; and American schoolchildren read Cooper's novels and thrill to stories of frontier life, pioneer days, and the Revolutionary War.

Although Cooper has always had his share of critics, none has ever been able to take away his greatest distinction as an author. When America was a brand new nation, struggling to forge a unique identity apart from Great Britain, when any author writing in America necessarily labored under the great shadow of British literary tradition, James Fenimore Cooper wrote about what he knew best— American people and American life. The man who at age thirty-one boldly declared to his family that he, with no experience as a writer, could improve upon a published work by an established author, also had the confidence to turn away from the tyranny of British cultural influences and help begin America's own literary tradition. In the words of critic Basil Davenport, written in an introduction to an edition of *The Last of the Mohicans*, "Cooper taught . . . his fellow countrymen . . . that their own wars and wilderness were a rich source of romance; and above all, that the rough, independent, resourceful American sailor or frontiersman is a hero worthy to stand beside the knights and cavaliers of the Old World."

FOR THE CHILDREN

Corn-Grinding Song

Zuñi Indians
Translated by Natalie Curtis

Yonder, yonder see the fair rainbow,
See the rainbow brightly decked and painted!
Now the swallow bringeth glad news to your corn,

Singing,
   "Hitherward, hitherward, hitherward, rain;
   Hither, come!"

Singing,
   "Hitherward, hitherward, hitherward, white
   cloud; Hither, come!"

Now hear the corn plants murmur,
   "We are growing everywhere!
   Hi, yai! The world, how fair!"

*Dressed in full regalia, LITTLE RAIN DANCER, painted by artist Donald
Zolan, is sure to bring a welcome shower. Image copyright ©
Zolan Fine Arts, Ltd., Hershey, Pennsylvania.*

Thanksgiving Prayer

Mamie Ozburn Odum

Lord, we thank Thee
For precious heritage our forefathers gave;
For noble ones so fearless, true, and brave
Who came to clear a wilderness unknown,
Transforming waste to a foundation stone,
Surviving dangers, loneliness, and fears,
Looking and trusting to the future years.
This day we lift our hearts, for we are free
To sing our songs of thanks, all thanks to Thee.
We thank Thee, Lord; this heritage we know
Has come to us through Thee, and so
In humbleness we lift our hearts in prayer,
Asking Thy protection and Thy daily care.
We thank Thee, Lord,
For food, shelter, hearth, home, and love,
For herds, new grain, and blessings from above.
As year by year we meet in festive scenes,
Help us to know just what Thanksgiving means.
And on this day of days in bright November,
Help us live true and heritage remember
And strive each year for better, nobler living,
Giving thanks to God on this Thanksgiving.

Artist Kathryn Andrews Fincher's touching painting evokes fond holiday remembrances of having a seat reserved at THE CHILDREN'S TABLE.
Image copyright © Arts Uniq, Cookeville, Tennessee.

The GATHERING

Loise Pinkerton Fritz

O Father of the harvest,
Hear this, our thankful prayer,
For all the precious gathering
Of bounty everywhere.

The sown seed has sprouted forth;
The full crop has appeared;
The wheat is garnered, tares cast off
For this, another year.

O Father of the harvest,
Keep us within Thy fold
That we may be the wheat, not tares,
At the gathering of souls.

THANKSGIVING PRAYER

Grace V. Watkins

For all the plenitude of joyous things
This year has brought, I offer thanks today.
But most for all the shining faith that sings
In my Thanksgiving heart. And oh, I pray
That while I lift my voice in gratitude
For all the glorious living I have had
This year, I shall remember, gracious God,
To say a thank You for the rich and glad
Abundance of the year that lies ahead.
And if somewhere along the trail of time
The hills and cliffs are steep that I must tread,
Oh, thank You, Father, for the strength to climb.

Two workers take a midday rest from their day in the fields in Harvesttime Near Holmbury Hill, Surrey *by artist George Vicat Cole (1833–1893). Image from Christie's Images.*

November

Della Adams Leitner

With shrieking laughter that his reign is here,
  The cold north wind sweeps down with
    stinging blasts
  And low to earth October's beauty casts.
Bare boughs in silhouette, all stark and sere
Accentuate with gloom the landscape drear.
  The hibernating furry folk whose fasts
  Are winter long now sink in sleep that lasts
Till warmth of spring calls verdure to appear.
But at the hearthside there is magic lure,
  A closeness and a coziness that brings
  Home hearts in unison with faith that sings
Of happiness and trust and love secure.

Fitting that thankfulness should be expressed
When chill November proves how we are blessed.

Requital in November

Dana Kneeland Akers

Down from a bare, untraveled space
Where a thousand miles of barrens run,
With a sting like a willow across the face
The north wind mocks a retreating sun.

But rough warm woolens resist the chill
In a pathless ramble through tawny wood.
There is odor of leaf fires on the hill;
There is zest of autumn, and life is good.

To the Country Born

Alice Mackenzie Swaim

It wears a kind identity,
This autumn wind that faintly reaches
The parched streets of the bustling city,
Hinting of harvest grapes and peaches;
Reminding all the country born
Of falling leaf and empty nest,
Proud pheasants feasting in the corn,
Harvest moon shining in the west.
May every heart it touches know
Blessing before the winter snow.

A windmill waits for the north wind to blow across a manicured farm in East Multnomah County, Oregon. Photo by Steve Terrill.

Country CHRONICLE
Lansing Christman

NOVEMBER SIESTAS

On these November days of sun, I journey to the meadows and woodlands for a familiar siesta, a siesta of reverie and meditation. I go to the fields and marshes to be surrounded by the soft winds and murmuring rills. I go to lose myself among the trees and grass, the reeds and songs.

Beneath the open November sky, I can escape from the hustle of the world around me. It matters not that the fields are brown and sere or that the days are shorter. For there, with the arms of nature around me, I am secure and I am at peace. Except for the evergreens, the trees are leafless; and a bright world seems to open before my eyes, a world with an infinite sky of vibrant blue.

As I breathe in the autumn afternoon, I enjoy watching the long threads of gossamers sparkling in the sun as they float from tree and fence and stubble. I do not mind that the delicate strands may pass lightly over my brow and face and hands, much as they did long years ago when I was following the plow through the November fields.

If I go to the swamp in the valley between the hills, I like to think of it as a cozy room where I can listen and dream. I smile as I hear the bell-like notes of the tree sparrows and the songs of the nuthatch and chickadees. The wind whispers in the ears of the reeds and cattails, and the red berries of the alder radiate in the mellow sunlight.

It is November. Loveliness rests upon the land where I seek my siestas in the sun.

The author of three books, Lansing Christman has contributed to Ideals for almost thirty years. Mr. Christman has also been published in several American, foreign, and braille anthologies. He lives in rural South Carolina.

A crimson barn rises among the golden leaves of a Wisconsin autumn.
Photo by Jessie Walker Associates.

Prayer of a Chippewa Indian

Author Unknown

O Father, whose voice I hear in the woods and whose breath gives life to all the world, hear me.

I am a man before you, one of Your many children. I am small and weak. I need Your strength and wisdom.

Let me walk in beauty, and make my eyes ever behold the red and purple sunsets. Make my hands respect the things You have made, my ears sharp to hear your voice.

Make me wise so that I may know the things You have taught my people, the lessons You have hidden in every leaf and rock.

I seek strength, Father—not to be superior to my brothers, but to be able to fight my greatest enemy, myself.

Make me ever ready to come to You with clean hands and a straight eye, so that when life fades like a fading sunset, my spirit may come to You without shame.

EARTH IS BUT THE FROZEN ECHO
OF THE SILENT VOICE OF GOD.
—SAMUEL MILLER HAGEMAN

The fall hues of Indian rhubarb are scattered along Indian Creek in Northern Sierra Nevada, California. Photo by Carr Clifton.

TREE PLANTING

Isla Paschal Richardson

The house was finished in the spring, too late
For planting shrubs and trees. The lawn must wait
In bare embarrassment until the fall.
Today the nurserymen at my call
Have come, and we are landscaping the place.
Small evergreens will fill the vacant space
Between nandinas and some others whose
Strange names escape me. And now I must choose
Locations for the trees. Ah, that takes thought!
Magnolias, dogwoods, and maples ought
To grow in careless order as if they
Came of their own accord, the casual way
Trees have of growing. Soft mimosas go
Beside my window—not too close—trees grow
And spread their graceful leaves further than we
Have calculated. Through this lacy tree
The sunset's rosy light will gleam on days
When I shall watch its disappearing rays.
Crabapple trees belong in southern clime,
And redbuds too to blossom in springtime.
This is the time for planting—late, late fall.
Grow little trees; grow strong and straight and tall
That some day in your shade children may play,
And I shall smile, remembering today.

He that planteth a tree is a servant of God.
He provideth a kindness for many generations,
And faces that he hath not seen shall bless him.
                          —*Henry van Dyke*

A new generation enjoys a long-ago planted tree in Floyds
Knobs, Indiana. Photo by Daniel Dempster.

A pine hutch and lantern exhibit two beautiful pierced-tin designs. Photo courtesy Country Accents, Williamsport, Pennsylvania.

PIERCED-TIN CABINET

Nan Senture

I have always loved the look of antique cabinets and hutches with pierced-tin panels. I have a space in my dining room that has been reserved for years for just the right such cabinet—a corner-shaped piece with four or five tiers of shelves to hold the dishes, glasses, and other odds and ends that are currently overflowing my limited kitchen space or packed away in boxes with nowhere else to go. I have toyed with the idea of buying an unfinished piece and painting it and adding the tin panels myself, but the process has always seemed beyond my talents, not to mention beyond the limits of my schedule. I have never had enough time to carefully and skillfully refinish something as large as a china

cabinet, nor to learn the skill of tin piercing. And since I have not found just the right cabinet at just the right price in my search of local antique shops and yard sales, the years have passed, my corner has remained bare, and my kitchen cabinets are still overflowing. This summer, however, my dream of a pierced-tin corner hutch came one step closer to reality, thanks to the kindness, generosity, and talent of a Pennsylvania artisan I met at a local country craft fair.

I did not go to the fair with the cabinet in mind, but it did not take long before I gravitated toward the furniture makers' booths and discovered a breathtaking display of pierced-tin art. The man responsible for the tin work was from Pennsylvania and had learned the craft, he told me, from his German grandfather. He was a friendly man and seemed ready to talk; and since it was early morning and the fair was still quiet, I sat down for a lesson on tin piercing.

As much as I had always admired the look of pierced tin, I had never given much thought to the purpose behind the rustic beauty of the finished product. This knowledgeable gentleman filled me in, and then some. He told me that tin piercing was centuries old and had developed to meet the needs of domestic life in the days before electricity and refrigeration. Pierced-tin lanterns allowed heat and light to escape while still keeping the flame within protected. And pierced-tin cabinets, my new friend told me, kept food ventilated and protected from insects.

As with most practical arts, tin piercing evolved into a decorative, expressive art in the hands of skilled artisans. The craft flourished first in Europe and then came to America with the Pennsylvania Dutch settlers. These hard-working families transformed the tin piercing they had learned at home into true American folk art. For hundreds of years, their patterns featuring hearts, tulips, and stars have been a cherished part of American country decor.

As I listened to the history of the craft, I looked around me at the examples wrought by this man's hands. I admired his wonderful collection of tin lanterns but was most impressed by his cabinetwork. He did not build his own furniture, but rather restored antiques, often replacing wooden cabinet doors with his own pierced-tin pieces. Other times he found old, damaged examples of pierced tin and brought them to new life with his own designs and skills. And among his wares was just the corner hutch of which I had dreamed. I went as far as measuring its dimensions to find that it would be a perfect fit for my corner. But before I took out my checkbook, I paused for one last inquiry. How difficult, I asked, would it be for a beginner to make something similar?

Wary of offending, I quickly added that, whereas I aspired to a similar piece, I in no way imagined I could produce the same quality as the work he displayed. I needn't have worried about offending him. This friendly artisan was thrilled at my interest in his craft and ready with a string of sug-gestions and encouraging words. He described to me the rather simple process of tin piercing, which today is done with tin plate rather than the very expensive pure tin found in antique pieces. Tin plate is sheet steel coated with tin and has a bright, durable finish that will not tarnish. The tin is cut to size with tin shears and then attached to a frame. Simple designs can be pierced directly onto the tin; more complex patterns should be done on graph paper, which is then taped to the tin piece and serves as a guide for piercing. The piercing itself, I learned, is done with a simple hammer and nails. It requires a steady, solid touch, one that becomes perfect with experience but can be picked up quickly enough by any eager student. All in all, he told me, if I could find the piece of furniture I wanted, I could make the tin panels.

Although I did ask that he hold onto the corner cabinet for awhile in case I changed my mind, all that I walked away with that day was a booklet of instructions with hastily written notes in the margins about materials and tools and methods. I also had a couple of book titles, some simple pattern sheets, the phone number of this wonderfully talented and generous man, and the confidence that a pierced-tin cabinet was a project that I could handle. I began hitting the local second-hand shops with a clear purpose—to find the corner hutch of which I have always dreamed, one that I could strip and paint and, finally, decorate with my own custom-made pierced-tin panels.

As I sat talking with this patient artisan, a man looking not to make a sale but to promote his craft, I realized that my excuse of insufficient time to refinish my own cabinet had been a weak one. As this clever gentleman pointed out, in all the years I had spent wishing and waiting to come upon the perfect piece, I could have slowly but surely produced my own. And, he asked, wouldn't it be so much more satisfying to look upon a pierced-tin cabinet that was the work not only of my wallet, but of my own hands? I couldn't agree more, and I can't wait to begin. Next summer, when this craft fair returns to our small town, I hope to find my friend from Pennsylvania and show him photographs of the lovely cabinet with pierced-tin panels standing in the corner of my dining room.

Family Recipes

An unexplained miracle of Thanksgiving is the way in which we each, after stuffing ourselves with triple servings of turkey and all the fixings, still eagerly reach for a slice of homemade pie. Next time you hear calls of "I couldn't eat another bite" from your holiday table, bring out one of the following pies and wait for the inevitable, "Well, maybe just a small slice, or two." Mail a typed copy of your own favorite recipe along with your name, address, and phone number to Ideals Magazine, ATTN: Recipes, 535 Metroplex Drive, Suite 250, Nashville, Tennessee 37211. We will pay $10 for each recipe chosen.

Peanut Butter Praline Pie
Mary L. Schmucker of New Paris, Indiana

Pie Crust
1½ cups vanilla wafer crumbs
3 tablespoons unsweetened cocoa
⅓ cup powdered sugar
6 tablespoons melted butter

Pie Filling
⅓ cup butter
¼ cup light brown sugar, packed
2 tablespoons granulated sugar
1 tablespoon cornstarch
2 tablespoons water
½ cup pecan pieces
1 3-ounce package vanilla pudding and pie mix
2 cups milk
2 cups peanut-butter chips
1 cup non-dairy whipped topping
Pecan halves for garnish

Preheat oven to 350° F. To make crust, in a large bowl, combine crumbs, cocoa, and powdered sugar. Add melted butter and mix thoroughly. Press mixture into bottom and up sides of a 9-inch pie pan. Bake 10 minutes. Set aside to cool.

In a small saucepan, melt ⅓ cup butter; remove from heat. Stir in brown sugar. In a small bowl, thoroughly mix granulated sugar with cornstarch. Add to brown sugar mixture with water, stirring well. Stir constantly over medium heat until mixture is bubbly; remove from heat. Stir in pecans. Pour mixture into cooled crust and refrigerate.

In a medium saucepan, combine pudding mix and milk. Stir constantly over medium heat until mixture boils. Immediately add peanut-butter chips; stir constantly until melted and well blended. Place plastic wrap directly onto surface of filling; refrigerate 1 hour. Stir to soften, then fold in whipped topping. Carefully spread over pecan layer in crust. Place plastic wrap directly onto filling; chill overnight. Just before serving, garnish with additional whipped topping and pecans. Makes 8 servings.

Hickory Nut Pie

Darlene Timm of Wood Lake, Minnesota

3 eggs
1 cup dark corn syrup
1 cup granulated sugar

2 tablespoons butter, melted
1 teaspoon vanilla
⅛ teaspoon salt

1 cup hickory nuts (or walnuts)
1 unbaked 9-inch pie crust

Preheat oven to 350° F. In a medium bowl, beat eggs lightly. Add next 5 ingredients, mixing well. Fold in nuts. Pour mixture into crust. Bake 55 minutes or until knife inserted in middle of pie comes out clean. Cool. Makes 8 servings.

Mystery Pie

Naomi Dyer of Eaton, Colorado

3 large egg whites
1 cup granulated sugar
1 teaspoon vanilla

1 teaspoon baking powder
20 round butter-flavored
  crackers, crushed

1 cup chopped pecans
Non-dairy whipped topping
Pecan halves for garnish

Preheat oven to 350° F. In a large bowl, beat egg whites until stiff. Stir in sugar, vanilla, and baking powder. Fold in crushed crackers and pecans, reserving a few pecans for topping. Pour into a greased 9-inch pie pan. Bake 25 minutes. Cool. Cover with whipped topping and refrigerate 3 hours. Garnish with additional pecan halves before serving. Makes 8 servings.

Cheddar Crust Apple Pie

Elsie Pattee of Union Mills, Indiana

1 recipe 9-inch, double-crust pie
1 cup grated mild Cheddar
  cheese, divided
4 Granny Smith apples

4 Jonathan apples
2 tablespoons butter, softened
½ cup plus 3 tablespoons
  granulated sugar, divided

½ cup brown sugar, packed
½ teaspoon ground cinnamon
½ cup all-purpose flour
2 tablespoons butter, melted

Place the first pie crust into a pie pan and sprinkle with ½ cup cheese. Set aside.

Preheat oven to 350° F. Peel, core, and slice apples; set aside. In a large bowl, combine butter, ½ cup granulated sugar, brown sugar, cinnamon, and flour until well blended. Fold in apples until well covered with sugar mixture. Spoon into prepared crust. Sprinkle remaining cheese over apples.

Unroll second pie crust over apples. Press edges to seal, and cut slits in top of pie. Brush top with melted butter and sprinkle with remaining sugar. Bake 45 minutes or until apples are soft and crust is golden brown. Allow to cool before cutting. Makes 8 servings.

A Kitchen Prayer

Betty W. Stoffel

Because my hands must be confined
And duty-bound within this place,
Set heavenly windows in my mind
And give me eyes for larger space.

Grant wings to thought, and set it free
To rise and blend and circle high
And move with God in majesty
Across the heights of holy sky

Until these hands hold deeds divine
And humble work is work for Thee,
Until this presence that is mine
Links labor with infinity.

May earthly deeds find heavenly grace,
May duty find a soul to bless,
May I, amid the commonplace,
Find service wrapped in godliness.

*A gingham-curtained window sheds light on
a farmhouse kitchen in Michigan. Photo by
Jessie Walker and Associates.*

My Kitchen Window

Andrea L. Johnson

When I ponder God's great gifts
With which my life is blessed,
I count my kitchen window
As perhaps one of the best.
I watched my children play and grow
While I scrubbed pots and pans.
I watched spring rains and autumn leaves
And dreamed of future plans.
There aren't as many dishes now;
My little boys are men.
But looking out my window,
I'm reminded once again,
God gives us ways of seeing things
We otherwise might miss,
Like kitchen windows bidding us,
"Slow down and look at this."

TRAVELER'S
Diary

CULINARY ARCHIVES AND MUSEUM
PROVIDENCE, RHODE ISLAND

Michelle Prater Burke

I consider myself to be an adequate cook when I try to be; and though I have less time for browsing through my cookbooks than I would like, I do occasionally attempt a new recipe, often to be stymied by a list of heretofore unheard-of ingredients and strange gadgets. After a recent visit to the Culinary Archives and Museum in Providence, Rhode Island, I was reminded that the joys and frustrations that I experience in my kitchen are as old as history itself.

The Culinary Archives and Museum was established in 1979 and consists of over half a million pieces of culinary memorabilia. Displayed in a cavernous warehouse at Johnson and Wales University in Providence, Rhode Island, the museum's priceless holdings have earned it the title the "Smithsonian Institution of the Foodservice Industry." Through an astounding variety of menus, recipes, tableware, tools, appliances, recipes, cookbooks, and more, the Culinary Archives offers a unique history of civilization through food.

Upon arriving at the museum, I was first taken to the cookbook collection, which numbers thirty thousand. In fact, the museum's first acquisition was a gift of 7,500 volumes, some dating back to the sixteenth century. In 1989, renowned chef Louis Szathmary expanded the museum's holdings with his gift of 400,000 culinary items and books. These and other donations allowed the museum to become more than just a library and to display such collections as a century-long history of the stove in life-size cast iron. When visiting the display, French chef Julia Child once paused sentimentally in front of a 1909 model, which she explained was the stove on which she had learned to cook as a child.

I moved from appliances to letters, eager to glimpse into the life of the notables through food-related correspondence signed by emperors, kings, presidents, and explorers. I was especially intrigued by the display honoring memorabilia of the U.S. Presidents, dubbed the "First Stomach" collection by the curator. Many of the items offer a humorous touch, including George Washington's newspaper ad for a White House cook, an ad which requested only those with "indubitable testimonials of sobriety, honesty, and attention" apply; and a letter from Thomas Edison attesting that his powers of invention were not the result of a fad vegetable diet.

The museum's historic objects are by no means limited to American pieces, however, nor to just the last few hundred years. Early antiquity is represented by such items as a five-thousand-year-old Scythian bronze trade knife; two A.D. 79 bakers' rings used to stamp dough; and a drinking vessel that dates from the time of Christ. Through the centuries, the story of food is told through everything from the ordinary—such as thousands of wooden spoons, the world's most popular cooking implement—to the unusual, represented by such oddities as a goose feather brush designed to spread butter on apple strudel.

By the time I was only halfway through my tour, I had already learned of the evolution of the chef's uniform, viewed elegant table settings from Chicago's finest turn-of-the-century hotel, and discovered a china cup designed to keep a gentleman's moustache dry while he drinks. The museum's

Some of the treasures from the Culinary Archives and Museum include A.D. 79 bakers' rings from Pompeii (opposite page); an 1849 cherry pitter, a nut grinder from the 1900s, and an 1880 cherry stoner (all above); and twentieth-century tools for making a favorite American treat, ice cream (at right).

thousands of illustrations and advertisements provide a glimpse into products long forgotten (such as Johnston's Fluid Beef, a seasoning sold around 1900) along with favorites, such as Quaker Oats, that have remained household staples for more than a century. One 1864 engraving depicting a railroad station's busy dining room was used to illustrate the origin of the word *tip*—To Improve Promptness. Gratuities were then offered before a meal, and one's generosity ensured quick service.

Throughout my tour, I found myself asking the guide question after question on the background of certain items, yet he seemed undaunted. I was told that the museum is used to receiving constant inquiries from chefs, writers, and researchers needing specialized information about historic table settings, recipes, or banquet menus. The curator has answered everything from a well-known producer's inquiries into how to replicate an 1870s high-society dinner, to questions from a Virginia restaurant on what First

Lady Martha Washington might have served for a picnic lunch at her Mount Vernon home.

As I returned home that evening after my fascinating walk through culinary history, I smiled when I unintentionally began wondering what to cook for dinner. I suppose mankind's age-old quest for a good meal continues, along with our determination to find the perfect tool to assist us, whether it be a raisin seeder or a sausage press. Perhaps next time I'm searching for a can of lychees (of which the grocer has never heard), I'll call the Culinary Archives and Museum for some guidance. I'm sure they would be able to offer an eighteenth-century menu to accompany the dish, and, with any luck, I just might get to borrow the perfect lychee slicer too.

THANKSGIVING FESTIVAL

Inez Franck

The woods are warm with red and yellow leaves
As wild geese fly and ripe persimmons fall;
The swift fox hurries from a hunter's chase
While goldenrod flings down an autumn shawl.

The peppers hang in strings upon the walls,
And gourds reflect the sun of mellow days;
The coon is out beneath the cheese-full moon
While hearthsides flicker with a fire-wood blaze.

The cornfield pumpkins line the kitchen shelves
Where cider smells of trees that bees embrace;
It's time to roast the turkey luscious-brown
And gather in our homes for special grace.

A family arrives home for the holidays in TURKEY ON THE RUN
by American artist Linda Nelson Stocks.

SALT AND PEPPER SHAKERS

Michelle Prater Burke

My grandmother always said her busy hands left her little time for words; she chose to speak to her family through her dinner table instead. Granny had accumulated a plethora of kitchen collectibles and tableware; and as a child, I could always tell her mood by what she chose for the table setting that day. For afternoons when Granny was in a fun-loving mood and her grandchildren were visiting, the table was set with bandanna napkins and whimsical salt and pepper shakers shaped like dachshund dogs. When she was feeling fancy and serving an elegant meal, we ate from a table laden with linen napkins, the good china, and crystal salt and pepper shakers.

But on the grandchildren's birthdays, Granny let the guest of honor decide on the table setting. Not only were we able to request our favorite meal, but we were also allowed to choose our favorite napkins, dishes, flowers, and, most exciting, any set of salt and pepper shakers from Granny's forty or so sets. A week before my birthday each year, I would begin planning which pair I would choose. Some years I selected a novelty set, such as one pair shaped like favorite nursery rhyme characters. As I began to feel more grown-up, I opted for a set which I felt displayed my newfound sophistication, such as a pair of ceramic shakers hand-painted with tiny rosebuds. Whatever my mood or age, Granny's salt and pepper shaker collection offered the right selection.

Displayed on the middle shelf of her cupboard, the myriad shapes and colors of the collection gleamed through the glass doors like a frozen carnival attraction, and I enjoyed pressing my nose against the doors to stare at the unexpected little figures, all standing in their proper pairs. Mostly made of glass and ceramic, the salt and pepper shakers were forbidden to a child with slippery fingers, unless it was time to season your corn. But on Saturdays when Granny dusted each piece, she would grin and hand over a feather duster and a pair of nodders (rocking sets with a stationery base) and allow me to bob them to and fro.

The years passed, and the grandchildren all moved on to kitchens of our own. Of us all, I was the one who inherited my grandmother's knack for cooking; yet I was still surprised when Granny arrived at my doorstep with a box that held her entire collection of salt and pepper shakers. Granny was still a woman of few words, and she quickly explained that she was tired of all that dusting and thought I might take over for a while. That evening, I dusted each pair carefully (taking time to play with the nodders) before placing it in my china cabinet.

My grandmother's collection, now my own, has grown unintentionally, beginning with a trip to an antique store, where I stumbled upon a glass shaker set featuring a pansy design. I thought innocently enough that the set would be a nice one-time complement to my collection. But since then, I seem to find excuses to purchase more and more "complements," from a bear-shaped novelty set that delights my teddy-loving preschooler to a pair of silver-inlay art glass shakers I purchased at a tag sale for a mere pocketful of change.

Granny still makes my favorite meal for my birthday each year, and I always bring my latest salt and pepper shakers for her to see. She examines them approvingly and states simply that I always was a good duster. She may not elaborate on her feelings, but I know she is pleased that I have taken up her former hobby. Granny's collection continues to grow under my roof, since each new pair I spot for sale seems to offer its own intriguing personality. I suppose this ability to appreciate uniqueness is the true lesson I learned from my grandmother. In her limited words, she taught me the sacredness of family dinnertime and the importance of celebrating the unique qualities of each meal, each day, and each family member. As I look at my young children, I wonder which pieces of my salt and pepper shaker collection will be their favorites one day. Just like Granny, I hope to have not only the ideal pair to join them for birthday dinners, but also the perfect set to give each day its special flavor.

A PINCH OF INFORMATION

If you would like to collect salt and pepper shakers, the following information may be helpful.

HISTORY

• Salt, which had long been a precious commodity, was served for centuries in special dishes such as salt cellars and standing salts. Several developments led to the evolution of the modern salt shaker, including scientific discoveries making salt more damp-proof and free-flowing in the 1800s, and the invention of the screw-top jar in 1858 by John Mason.

• Until the 1890s, shakers were still commonly referred to as *dredges*, *spice boxes*, or numerous other names.

• The salt shaker was first partnered with the pepper shaker during the Civil War, when a patent was given on two small cylinders with metal lids.

• In the late nineteenth century, improved land transportation and a fast-growing population increased the demand for attractive glassware and fine art glass shakers in America.

• Novelty sets have two different but related shakers, many of which replicate humans or animals. These figural sets rose in popularity from the 1920s to the 1950s.

• By the 1960s, ceramic and glass shakers had been replaced by inexpensive plastic sets in most homes.

• Though once considered only a "poor man's collectible," salt and pepper shakers are now available in a wide range of prices. Although the majority of sets can still be purchased for only a few dollars, designs in high demand can sell for thousands of dollars.

NARROWING A COLLECTION

Such a wide variety of salt and pepper shakers is available today that many collectors are able to accumulate hundreds or even thousands of pairs. Other collectors choose to focus on one or more specific areas of interest, including:

Hand-painted salt and pepper shakers such as those above are traditional additions to a collection. Photo by Jessie Walker.

• Traditional crystal, glass, or silver sets.

• Sought-after Japanese sets.

• Sets from a single designer or manufacturer, such as Ceramic Arts Studio or Rosemeade.

• Art glass sets, which include bristol glass and Bohemian glass.

• Two-in-one or combination shakers which combine salt and pepper shakers in one piece.

• Novelty sets associated with a theme, such as water, nursery rhymes, or animals.

• Groups of novelty shaker sets that were manufactured in a series.

• Small individual shakers sold in sets of six or more to be used at each place setting.

• Plastic shakers produced as advertising premiums in the 1950s. These sets often replicated the newest appliances of the day, such as miniature toasters, mixers, or rotisseries.

Remember When

ALL DOORS LED TO THE KITCHEN

Marjorie Holmes

I am a modern woman, and my kitchen is my pride. I'm glad I don't have to build a fire in the cookstove or nag a son to carry out the ashes. . . . But I warmly recall the days of the big, smelly, noisy, inconvenient kitchen, short on cupboard space but long on living. Days when the kitchen was the family room, hub and heart of the house.

All doors led inevitably back to the enormous teeming kitchen. For here practically every activity occurred—cooking, eating, reading, washing, ironing, playing games, and sometimes sleeping, for it wasn't uncommon for the kitchen to include a couch.

Undisputed queen of this kitchen was the big black range. It warmed you, cooked your meals, heated your bath water and the flatirons with which your mother ironed your clothes. The day always started with the stove. There was the pound of feet on the back stairs as Dad or a brother went down to cope with it. The rattle of shaken ashes, the crack of kindling, the click of lids, the clatter of coal—such was the first music of morning. By the time the kids had been hounded out of bed, grabbed their clothes and dashed downstairs to dress, the teakettle would be rocking and spitting, the coffee boiling richly in its chipped granite pot, and the fragrance of thick bacon or side meat filling the house.

Second only in importance to the kitchen stove was the kitchen table. No breakfast nooks for us, no perching on stools at a snack bar. Instead, just as the stove drew you with its warmth, the table drew you to its broad, hospitable bosom. A huge walnut table, usually, sometimes round, sometimes square, and covered with oilcloth.

Here, rushing in after school, you found your mother kneading the slippery, squeaky white bread dough, or setting out the tall brown, heavenly smelling loaves to cool. Or she would be rolling out piecrust or pitting cherries for canning. Whatever her labors, there was always room to spread out your books, your kites, your paper dolls, or your treasures of rocks and leaves and wildflowers. Here, munching whatever it was she was cooking, the two of you visited.

By some legerdemain our mother managed to remove all this and set that same table for supper if Dad wasn't home. (When he was, or if we had company, she used the dishes from the glass china closet instead of the pantry, and we ate in the dining room.) And afterward, she got the dishpans off the nails on the back porch, and there too the dishes were washed. Then when all this was cleared away, the real activities of the evening began:

The homework—the singsong of multiplication tables, the drill on spelling words accompanied by a little chorus of outdoor sounds. Crickets and katydids beyond the screen, a barking dog. Rain at the windows, or the soft, almost audible silence of snow. Or wind that rattled shutters, made the panes squeal with dancing branches, and puffed the rag rugs Mother had put against the doorsills to keep it out. All of this sheltered and cupped in the kitchen, still steamy and redolent of supper, with the range clucking and whispering away like a companionable old nanny.

Somebody always got hungry, and there was always a discussion whether to stir up the fire and add more fuel, or let it die down and use the coals. We made a batch of fudge, which bubbled richly until the precise moment when it "spun a thread," then was beaten lengthily on the cold, enclosed back porch and cut in mealy squares and served still in the buttery pie tin. Or cups of scalding black cocoa, with marshmallows melting in a foamy gum on top. Or we toasted the marshmallows, which Dad brought home in a striped candy sack, over the rosy intensity of the coals.

A mother and children gather around the stove to preview the evening meal. Image from Superstock.

Sometimes we roasted apples in these fiercely glowing pink coals. The coals were marvelous for toasting bread, too. You pinioned it on a long-handled fork, held it, standing back, until the sudden instant of its golding. A second longer might burn it into a cinder—but to snatch it back and butter it now meant perfection. The outside crisp, the inside tender, and the whole of it subtly flavored with the breath of fire.

The most frequent treat was popcorn. The sound and the smell of the white imps dancing as if eager to join us added to our pleasure. You could see them jumping to get out. Then when the popper could hold no more they were released into a dishpan, slathered with salt and butter, and eaten by the handful.

Certainly at night parents were not always off at parties or meetings. Mostly they too were home—and not off in a basement workshop, or immersed in papers at a desk, or absorbed in their hobbies, but in the big sprawling kitchen where everybody gravitated. And to exclude them from your activities would be unthinkable. In fact, if they did actually prefer to read or sew or attend to other pursuits we were shocked and grieved. Didn't they appreciate our fascinating company? We knew that without theirs we felt deprived. For when night fell and the supper dishes were cleared away, it was as if a kind of happy magic invaded the house, and its focus was the kitchen table. There Mother seemed to shed her cares along with her apron. She became lively, pretty—even witty. And that worried and often grim authority, Dad, turned into an outright clown. . . .

I sometimes wish that we could all be whisked back together in time. That my children would have to chop wood, haul water, build a fire before they could eat or bathe or even have clean clothes. Above all, I wish they could draw their chairs into the snug circle around the kitchen table after supper, when the day's chores were done and everybody was ready for fudge and popcorn. Ready for the comfort and pleasure of each other's company, while the wind snooped round the door and the rosy coals of the old cookstove clucked like a benediction on the grate.

Applewood
Ruth B. Field

The apple log upon the still air lays
Its fragrance, drifting through the quiet room,
And in the flickering crimson golden blaze
Returns aroma of its springtime bloom.
Once it reached gnarled hands toward the sky,
Absorbed the crystal offerings of rain,
Saw spring and summer softly drifting by,
Upon it winter's ermine long has lain.
Safely confined, small holocaust so bright,
A dream, perhaps, of fragrant blossomed crest,
Gave rest to birds returned from distant flight,
And gently held each interwoven nest.
Do you recall the children 'neath your boughs,
The happy laughter in your sheltering shade,
The romance of young lovers' whispered vows,
Your rosy fruit dropped in the grassy glade?
Oh, Maytime lives within your glowing embers
And echoes in your flames like melodies
Warm the heart as it fondly remembers
Your smoke-dreams rise like fragrant melodies.

Hearth Fires
May Allread Baker

I love a fire of applewood
These crisp, autumnal nights.
The leaping flames of rainbow hues
Shame artificial lights.

While in their last and final fling,
These old logs must, I think,
Go back to days when they were young
With blossoms white and pink.

And spend themselves in going out
With beauty as they burn,
While bright sparks up the chimney fly
To nevermore return.

Let others seek out gala spots
Or on the highways roam;
I'll take my fire of applewood
Upon the hearth at home.

A seamstress enjoys a peaceful fireside in SEWING BY THE FIREPLACE *by artist Marguerite Stuber Pearson. Image from Christie's Images.*

Landmarks

Rose Koralewsky

How drab (you would say) is this road!
Dead branches, dead leaves, and dead grass.
Monotonous—yes, without end.
But could you revisit with me
The landmarks my memory holds,
Each step would be sheerest delight.

These capsules all lacquered in brown
Are massed where the red lilies bloom,
Their gay, flaring trumpets aglow
With summer's own essence of life.
In August, along this small brook,
The curious turtlehead grows;
White flowers, with lavender streaked,
Sway gently amid the long grass.

Just pause by this little gray swamp.
One memorable day in mid-June
I first found the pitcher plant here,
Its tall freakish blossoms of red,
Its strange goblin-pitchers of green.
Here too is pogonia hid—
A frail rosy flower, so small
It scarce can be seen in the bog.
Down there in that thicket I've watched
A Luna moth drying its wings
Of almost ethereal green.

Like moonlight on midsummer seas
All over that high sloping bank
An exquisite wild orchid grows.
What heavenly sweetness exhales
From each little waxen white bell!

Invisible landmarks are these,
And yet the keen eye of the mind
Discerns them—and lo! the dull road
Is vibrant with color and life.

A country lane passes through a woodland of gold in Hudson, Massachusetts. Photo by William Johnson/Johnson's Photography.

BITS & PIECES

If the world is cold, make it
your business to build fires.
—*Horace Traubel*

*T*he child says nothing but
what is heard by the fire.
—*Author Unknown*

*I*n the face of the sun you may see
God's beauty; in the fire you may feel
His heart warming.

—*Jeremy Taylor*

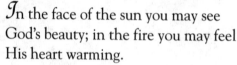

*N*ow stir the fire and close the shutters fast,
Let fall the curtains, wheel the sofa round. . . .
So let us welcome peaceful evening in.
—*William Cowper*

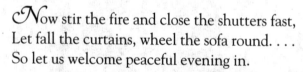

*F*ire is the most tolerable third party.
—*Henry David Thoreau*

*B*y the fireside still the light is shining,
The children's arms round the parents twining.
From love so sweet, oh, who would roam?
Be it ever so homely, home is home.

—*Dinah Maria Mulock*

The cozy fire is bright and gay;
The merry kettle boils away
And hums a cheerful song.
I sing the saucer and the cup;
Pray, Mary, fill the teapot up,
And do not make it strong.
—*Barry Pain*

Duty done is the soul's fireside.
—*Robert Browning*

Burn bright, fire;
Sparks, leap higher!
Your warmth for hands,
Your joy for hearts,
Comfort and cheer
To all imparts.
—*Lucile Waer*

How great a matter a little fire kindleth.
—*James 3:5*

All our adventures were by the fireside.
—*Oliver Goldsmith*

To make a happy fireside clime
To weans and wife,
That's the true pathos and sublime
Of human life.
—*Robert Burns*

In Autumn

Louise Weibert Sutton

Out where the southbound mallards fly,
Blue woodsmoke curls against the sky
As over hills of lazy herds
Wheel other flocks of southbound birds.
The evening mists more closely fold
Across the mapled hills of gold,
And farms that stud the old earth's brow
Are harvest-piled with pumpkins now.

Tall asters by the garden fence
Their blue-mound beauty now commence.
Before the frosty ending comes,
They view with bright chrysanthemums.
At evening homebound children race,
Each with a wind-flushed, smiling face,
From ordered classrooms' final bells
To kitchens filled with cookie smells.

The air is sweet as amber wine,
Such fragrance simply is divine,
As apples in the orchard-sun
Invite small boys to sample one.
Along the road each wayside stand
Has cider jugs on every hand.
(If I could bottle autumn's air
It would outsell the cider there!)

Let poets sing of April boughs
Or springtime's warmly whispered vows,
Of summer's amber-hearted charms
And August's green-clad, circling arms.
I still prefer, above them all,
The feel of harvest-home in fall
When heated sun and glare depart
For things more gentle to the heart.

*A farmstand in Wolfeboro, New Hampshire, offers a tempting array
of fall treasures. Photo by William Johnson/Johnson's Photography.*

Readers' Forum

Phyllis L. Sizemore of Fairdale, West Virginia, loves to dote on her grandchildren. Pictured top left, four-year-old Thomas Mark Covey, son of Thomas and Tammy Covey, displays his climbing ability while on a trip to a state park last November. Six-year-old Kaylee Lynn Prichard, pictured middle left, is posing among the autumn decor in Grandma Phyllis's yard last year. Kaylee is the daughter of Jeffery and Kathy Prichard.

Frances B. Russell of Greenville, South Carolina, sent *Ideals* this snapshot, below, of her great-granddaughters Susannah and Mary Bradley Pazdan. The twins, who are the daughters of Emilie and John Pazdan, delighted everyone when they dressed as pink- and purple-skirted ballerinas for Halloween last year.

Thank you Phyllis L. Sizemore, Frances B. Russell, Mrs. Dollie Ruth Mincy, Joan M. Epps, and Sherry Rast for sharing your family photographs with *Ideals*. We hope to hear from other readers who would like to share snapshots with the *Ideals* family. Please include a self-addressed, stamped envelope if you would like the photos returned. Keep your original photographs for safekeeping and send duplicate photos along with your name, address, and telephone number to:

Readers' Forum
Ideals Publications
535 Metroplex Drive, Suite 250
Nashville, Tennessee 37211

Nine-year-old Hannah Shipman, pictured above, is dressed as a Pilgrim and ready for her fourth-grade class's Thanksgiving play. Her costume perfectly suits her posing in front of the spinning wheel on which her great-great-grandmother once spun wool. This snapshot of Hannah was sent to us by her great-great-aunt, Mrs. Dollie Ruth Mincy of Kerrville, Texas.

Joan M. Epps of Richmond, Virginia, shares this photo, at right, of her grandson, four-year-old Richard Thomas Williams, as he poses in his grandmother's hat among her beautiful fall flowers. Richard Thomas is the son of Dana and Richard Williams.

Two farmhands are better than one; at least that is what Zachary Aschenberg (left) and Lucas Rast (right) have discovered. Lucas's mother, Sherry Rast of Highlands Ranch, Colorado, sent us this photo of the two toddler buddies, who were visiting Littleton Historical Museum in Littleton, Colorado. The living history museum is a working farm with employees in period costumes—the perfect backdrop for Lucas and Zachary's harvest chores.

ideals

Publisher, Patricia A. Pingry
Editor, Michelle Prater Burke
Designer, Travis Rader
Copy Editor, Elizabeth Kea
Editorial Assistant, Amy Johnson
Contributing Editors, Lansing Christman, Deana Deck, Pamela Kennedy, and Nancy Skarmeas

ACKNOWLEDGMENTS

CARMICHAEL, AMY. "Autumn" from *Toward Jerusalem.* Copyright © The Dohnavur Fellowship 1936, published by Christian Literature Crusade, Fort Washington, PA 19034. Used by permission. HOLMES, MARJORIE. An excerpt from "All Doors Led to the Kitchen" from *You and I and Yesterday.* Used by permission of the author. KORALEWSKY, ROSE. "Landmarks" from *New England Heritage & Other Poems.* Used by permission of Branden Publishing. ODUM, MAMIE OZBURN. "Thanksgiving Prayer" from *Heart Leaves.* Used by permission. OLSON, ENID MARTELL. "A Church Spire" from *Poems of Faith.* Reprinted from *Poems of Faith* by Enid Martell Olson, Copyright © 1959, Augsburg Publishing House. Used by permission of Augsburg Fortress. RICHARDSON, ISLA PASCHAL. "Thanksgiving" from *Along the Way* and "Tree Planting" from *Against All Time.* Used by permission of Branden Publishing. STOFFEL, BETTY W. "A Kitchen Prayer" from *Moments of Eternity.* Used by permission. TABER, GLADYS. "October" from *Stillmeadow Calendar.* Copyright © 1967 by Gladys Taber. Reprinted by permission of Brandt & Brandt Literary Agents, Inc. Our sincere thanks to the following authors and publishers whom we were unable to locate: May Allread Baker for "Gathering Pawpaws" from *The Gift of the Year,* Brethren Press; May Allread Baker for "Hearth Fires"; Ethelyn M. Crawford for "Autumn Festival" from *Bower of Quiet;* Sudie Stuart Hager for "Thanksgiving Inventory" from *Earthbound;* Berniece Ayers Hall for "Torches"; Bertha A. Kleinman for "Thanksgiving" from *Through the Years;* Anya P. Sala for "In Autumn, Fruits"; May Smith White for "Autumn's Beauty" from *Forty Acres;* and for Lucile Waer for quotation from "Verse for a Fireplace" from *Leaves in the Wind.*